SIENA
Town of art

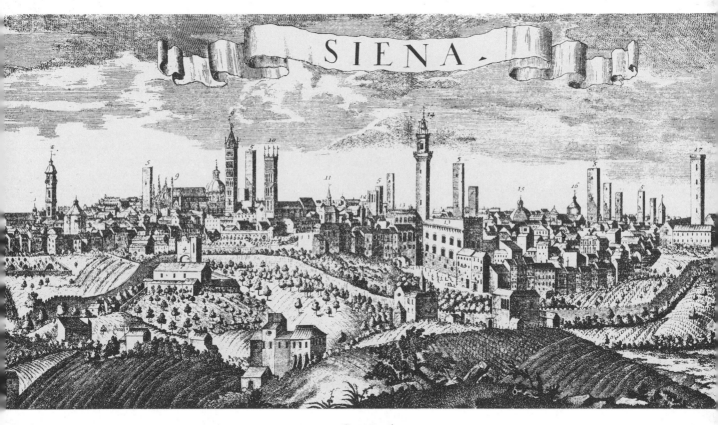

ESCLUSIVISTA DI VENDITA
PER LA TOSCANA
ROMBONI MARIO
Via Battisti, 20 - Tel. 283263
SIENA

Edito e stampato dalla

plurigraf
Narni - Terni

Siena, town of art

The tourist who goes along the modern road leading to Siena from Florence, sees all around himself a very pleasant landscape, rich in green fields of olive-trees, vineyards and cypresses. The medieval and characteristic towers of S. Gemignano rising on the right side, near Poggibonsi, tell us that Siena is near. The lanscape looks quite different to those who reach the town through the south of the province by the Cassia or Valdichiana roads. This side of the country, though bare in some of its parts, presents characteristic and suggestive features, thanks mainly to its picturesque clays and hills of clay with their corn-fields. On top of these hills there is always a tree, as if it were a sort of plume.

Siena was a Roman colony during the Republican age. During the imperial age and the early Middle ages, it went through many terrible events. Its expansion, however, was always limited by the greater power and rivalry of Florence. Being far from the sea and open only towards the lands of the Maremma, Siena was often besieged and devastated and had to face civil wars and terrible pestilences.

After the domination of the Longobards and Franks, it passed under the Bishop-Counts, towards the middle of the XIth century. Then there was the turn of the Consuls, with a lay government. And it was in this period that Siena reached the height of its political and economic power, specially after the famous battle of Montaperti in 1260, by which it defeated the Florentines. Arts and culture flourished in this time. Thanks mainly to the Government of the Nine, which, restored in 1277, ruled for about 70 years, the magnificents monuments of Siena were built during this period of time. The renowned « Piazza del Campo » is its most precious pearl and the centre of its peculiar town-planning. This square, with its famous buildings, is the spacious and resounding shell, where the city-life takes place. It is the suggestive amphitheatre, whose background is constituted only by the « Palazzo Pubblico » with the Tower of Mangia, the best example of the 14th century civil architecture. The characteristic medieval look of Siena dates back to the same century. The town has kept its original look. In its streets made of bricks and stones, among the high buildings, adorned with elegant three-mullioned windows and slender ogive arches, in the suggestive courtyards, in the closed and dark entrance halls, in the narrow alleys and squares, you perceive a sort of ancient atmosphere, which makes Siena so charming.

It is a medieval town, but mostly a town of art. If one is intensely excited at the sight of the Campo, one is amazed at the sight of the monuments of the town, the Cathedral and the other churches, the museums. Everywhere one finds precious masterpieces, wonderful works of Nicola and Giovanni Pisano, Duccio and Simone Martini, Donatello and Ghiberti, who have left here some examples of their immortal art.

Painting, which was the most genuine and significant expression of the creativeness of the Sienese, new architectonic ideas and an original school of sculpture, one of the best in Italy, more refined technics in gold working and designs, made of Siena one of the greatest leader in the field of art in Italy and Europe, since the end of the 13th century and the early 14th century. If in the 14th century the Sienese art reached its height with Duccio and Simone Martini, Pietro and Ambrogio Lorenzetti, we must not forget that during the two next centuries the figurative arts reached very high levels, thanks to artists like Jacopo della Quercia, Sassetta, Sano di Pietro, Giovanni di Paolo, just to mention a few. When in the 17th century the Town of Siena declined because of internal divisions and the decreasing richness of its merchants and bankers and so was overcome by the rising power of Florence and annexed to the Grand Duchy of Tuscany, its people took refuge, as it were, in the glories of the past, in its institutions and greatest memories.

Being conscious of having a personality of their own, the Sienese people kept its love for the old districts, its civil and religious traditions, the Palio, which is something more than a horse-race. The Palio is a wonderful show commemorating the glory of the ancient Republic. It is a popular feast, which, since the Middle Ages, aroused people's enthusiasm. By the Palio, the Sienese express the feelings and passions of their 17 « contrade » or districts. And it is by this fight among the contrade that the ancient Siena goes on living together with the actual Siena, in the harmonious and suggestive atmosphere of a historical and artistic environment, which is unique in the world.

Piazza del Campo and Palazzo Pubblico

The peculiar shape of Piazza del Campo or simply « il Campo » (the Field) is due to the canalization and diversion of rain-waters on an irregular and bare ground, shaped like an amphitheatre, where the three hills, on which Siena rises, meet together. This happened during the 13th century. This square, however, is incomparably beautiful and the essential element of the Sienese town-planning. It is famous all over the world and unique in its kind. It looks like a shell, which shows the particular nature of the ground, harmonizing nature and art. It is paved along its borders, while the central part is made of bricks arranged like a fish-bone and divided into nine parts by white stone-strips, which commemorate the Rule of the Nine. At the base of the shell, as a sort of background on the wide cavea of the square, there is the Palazzo Pubblico (Public Palace), surrounded by remarkable buildings, with the slender Tower of Mangia, and, at its foot, the Cappella di Piazza (the Chapel of the Square). It is magnificent and elegant, simple and picturesque at the same time, in its structure and harmonious division of its area. It is the most renowned one of the Gothic-Tuscan buildings and the best example of the Sienese civil architecture, which, more than others, presents more slender lines and a peculiar. ornate style.

The history of this building is strictly connected with the political and economical affairs of Siena. It was begun in 1250, as records of that time show. In 1299 the central part was completed, while the building of the two wings was begun in 1305. In 1310 the Palazzo had the shape which it kept till in 1680 and at the beginning of the 18th century some other parts were added to its structure, though the stylistic unity of its front was kept. The front is made of stone in its lower part with the characteristics Sienese arches. The second and third storeys are made of bricks, with two orders of three-mullioned windows. A fourth storey, higher than the two side bodies, with small arches and merlons. Among the mullioned windows of this storey there is a large copper disk with the monogram of Christ, the symbol of St. Bernardine, and on the sides two stony she-wolves. The Palazzo Pubblico was once the seat of the Government and the Mayor of the ancient Sienese Republic. Today it is the seat of the Municipality.

FONTE GAIA – This fountain was built on the opposite side of the Palazzo Pubblico, where once a 14th century fountain was. It was made by Jacopo di Pietro, called « della Quercia », probably after Quercegrossa, his family's place, around Siena. This fountain is shaped like a rectangular basin, surrounded, on three sides, by a high parapet. It was made between 1409 and 1419. It looks like a magnificent altar made of white marbles, which anticipates some of the basic features of the Renaissance, with its strict connection between sculpture and architecture and plastic forms. Among the sculptures adorning the fountain in the centre, there is the image of the Madonna, surrounded by the Virtues and the Creation of Adam and Adam and Eve driven out of Eden. In 1858 the original reliefs were substituted with reproductions made by Tito Sarocchi and transferred into the Loggia of the Palazzo Pubblico.

PALAZZO PUBBLICO – a detail of the facade, with the flags of the 17 « contrade » of Siena during the Palio.

PALAZZO SANSEDONI – surmounted by a rhomb-shaped tower, this building, erected in the former part of the 13th century and enlarged in 1399, presents the same basic features of the Palazzo Pubblico, as other buildings of the Campo.

CAPPELLA DI PIAZZA – This Chapel, surmounted by the Tower of Mangia, was built to fulfill a vow made by the Sienese during the 1348 pestilence. It was begun in 1352 by Domenico d'Agostino and completed around 1376 by Giovanni di Cecco who completed also the pillars and the roof. In 1468 Antonio Federighi substituted the simple ceiling with the vault with the frieze of the owls and a cornice, matching so Renaissance elements to the Gothic style of the Chapel. On the pillars there are statues of saints, made by various sculptores, while some marbles, taken from another monument and partly re-shaped by Andrea Becheroni in 1846, adorn the parapets of the chapel. The wrought iron gates were made by Conte di Lelio Orlandi and Petruccio di Betto. Near the altar there is a fine fresco made by Sodoma, representing the « Madonna with Saints and the Eternal Father », unfortunately damaged.

10

PALAZZO PUBBLICO –
« The Mayor's Court-
yard » – One reaches
it by a door near the
Cappella di Piazza. It
was built in 1325 and
restored in 1929. It
consists of a portico
surmounted by a stor-
ey with a series of
large three-mullioned
windows. Along the
walls there are some
coat-of-arms of Mayors
and a fresco, badly
damaged and incomple-
te, dating back to
the 14th century and
representing the Ma-
donna and two angels.
In the photo: the rem-
ains of the statue of
« Mangia » and « The
She-wolf feeding the
twins », a golden tin
work of Giovanni di
Turino (1429-30), which
are in the vestibule
and at the end of the
portico.

THE TOWER OF MANGIA, seen from the Mayor's Courtyard. This slender tower, dominating the town, shows not only the architectonic genius but of the workers of that time but is also a great work of engineering. It is called so after Giovanni di Duccio, named « Mangiaguadagni » o more simply « Mangia », engaged by the Municipality to ring the bells. The automaton, which was put there to strike the hours on the tower till 1780, was called « Mangia ». The brick pipe was erected by the Aretine brothers Minuccio di Rinaldo and Francesco Naldi, under the direction of Giovanni d' Agostino (1338-1348).

After a very slender cornice, there is the firts travertine coping, with two coat-of-arms of the Municipality, with a rampant lion in the middle, then the bell-tower made on designs of Lippo Memmi (1341). Above it there is the big bell cast in 1665 and called by the Sienese « Campanone » or « Sunto », because it was « christenëd » Maria Assunta.

The top of the tower is 88 metres high up to the last merlons and 102 up to the point of the lightning-conductor. One reaches it through the Mayor's Courtyard. From there one can enjoy a wonderful view on the whole town and the surrounding hills. Towards south-east (above, on the left) one can see the Basilica of S. Maria dei Servi, and, on the horizon, Mount Amiata. On a side one can see a corner of Piazza del Campo with Palazzo Sansedoni and, below, another sight of the town with the apse of the Cathedral, the belfry and the walls of the New Cathedral.

Piazza del Campo on a pleasant Spring morning: the shadows of the Palazzo Pubblico and the Tower of Mangia on the square and the nearby buildings suggestively reproduce the silhouette of the most famous Sienese building. It is famous because it is beautiful and represents the architectonic unity of the square. This building, however, is not connected with the square only from the artistic, but also historical, traditional and cultural points of view.

It was here that the Sienese, through the centuries, have faced the most important events of their history; it was here that they have rejoiced and suffered. If the Campo is the heart of Siena, the scenery of its past history and centre of its life, the Palazzo is the symbol of that history, the guardian of its dearest memories and cultural values. The noblest feelings of the people of Siena go on living in this square, which is the most important testimony of the extraordinary artistic and cultural development during the age of the Free Towns.

PALAZZO PUBBLICO - Interior — The Globe's Hall. The Globe's Hall, so called after a map painted in the 14th century by Ambrogio Lorenzetti and now lost, is situated on the first floor of the building, which houses now a Museum. On the walls of the smaller sides there are two magnificent frescoes of the « Maestà » and « Guidoriccio da Fogliamo » by Simone Martini. Above the arches, through which one gets into the Chapel and vestibule, there are monochromatic frescoes, and on the pillars images of Sienese Saints and Blessed. In the side photo, St. Catherine of Siena, by Vecchietta (1461). Below, a sight of the hall with the « Maestà » on the background. This is the first work which can be attributed to Simone Martini without any doubt. This artist was one of the greatest representatives of the 14th century painting. If, according to Vasari, he died in 1344, when he was 60, it means that he was born in 1284. Simone painted the « Maestà » in 1315. Six years after, however, he had to restore the fresco damaged by damp. Under a canopy supported by eight apostles, there is the Madonna with the Child, on a throne, surrounded by angels, saints and other apostles. A wide strip of 20 medallions with images of Christ, prophets and evangelists surrounds the composition. Below, in the centre, a double-faced figure represents the old an new laws and a medallion reproducing the seal of the Republic.

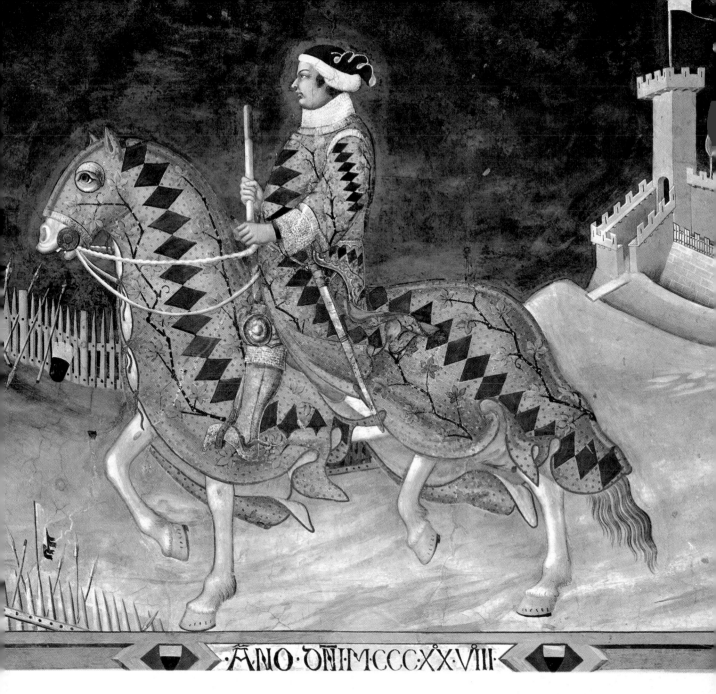

THE GLOBE'S HALL – « Guidoriccio da Fogliano ». On the opposite side, above, there is another fresco of Simone Martini, representing « Guidoriccio da Fogliano » after the victory over the Castles of Montemassi and Sassoforte of Maremma, which had rebelled in Siena in 1328. The work, completed in 1329, was a part of a series of representations of Castles conquered by the Sienese Republic. Unfortunately this work went lost. In the centre, the « condottiero » (leader), magnificentely paraded, proud and silent, triumphally going towards the conquered castles. This fresco is certainly one of the best and most famous works of Simone Martini. The vast scene presents a sort of monumental magnificence, with the towered castles on the background. It is really a poetic and heroic evocation of the event.

THE GLOBE'S HALL – A detail of the « Maestà ». It is considered the oldest fresco of the all Sienese painting. In this work Simone Martini combines the refined « French Gothic » style with Hellenistic elements taken from Duccio and new elements of the Italian art, represented by the Pisan sculptors and Giotto. The intense expressions of the characters, the delicate lines, the vivid volours, the refined details, all take you into another mystical reality.
In the pictures on this page: above, from left, a detail of the Virgin and Magdalen; below, S. Ansano and S. Crescenzio, who together with S. Vittore and Savino are the Patron Saints of Siena.

THE HALL OF PEACE or THE NINE – This hall is so called because it was the seat of the Government of the Nine. In it is kept the most famous cycle of secular frescoes of all the Sienese painting. It is one of the works of Ambrogio Lorenzetti of Siena (1319-1348), painted between 1337 and 1339.

The great political, didactic and moral representation consists of three parts: « The Allegory of the Good Government », which can be seen in the photo above; « The Results of the Good Government in the town and countryside », and « The Allegory and the Results of the Bad Government », below, all forming one composition. Unfortunately the latter one is badly damaged.

THE HALL OF PEACE OR THE NINE — « The Good Government » (a detail). « The Good Government » is represented by an old, solemn king dressed in white and black. These are the colours of the « Balzana », the Sienese flag, and the coat-of-arms of the town. On his left side, Justice, Temperance and Magnanimity; on his right side, Prudence, Fortitude and Peace. Above, the three theological virtues, while at the feet of the King the She-wolf feeds Aschius and Senius, sons of Remus and mythical founders of Siena. Below, « The Results of the Good Gouvernment in the town » (a detail): a view of the 14ht century Siena where, among towers and embattled buildings, various activities flourish, with elegant cavalcades along its streets, young dancers crowding the squares and streets of the town. Here are the harmoniously combined features of a society, which is happy thanks to the great virtues of the « Good Gouvernment ».

21

THE HALL OF PEACE – Another detail of the Results of the Good Gouvernment: a door on the city walls opens on to the countryside, where life pulses among farm-houses, castles, vineyards, woods and olive-groves. In the side picture: the dancers.

This is the most lively and interesting composition of the whole cycle. Lorenzetti describes here every-day life – the market, a cavalcade outside the gates, a lady dressed in red on a white horse, dancing girls. Each event, however, and each figure bear witness to the 14th century way of life and its deep and genuine values. It is so that the imposing conceptual and allegorical structure, based on the contrast between good and evil, the good and bad government, becomes poetry by a very original language.

And it is in this work that Ambrogio Lorenzetti reached his artistic ideal, which expresses itself in the perfect balance of all the values, between colour and volume, in the lines clearly marking mass and colour.

CHE RACCIETA CHE QVI FIGVRATA · 7 DSVA CIALECIA CORONATA · LAQVAL SEDRA

THE CHAPEL — Near the Globe's Hall there is a magnificent chapel, closed by an elegant wrought-iron gate, designed probably by Jacopo della Quercia and made in 1437 by the Sienese Giacomo di Vita and his son Giovanni. Above the marble altar of Marrina, there is a beautiful painting of Sodoma representing the « Holy Family and St. Leonard. On the vaults of the walls of the chapel there are frescoes made by Taddeo di Bartolo around 1407 and representing the Evangelists, the Doctors of the Church, various prophets and stories of the Virgin's life. Below, the funeral of the Madonna.

Along the walls of the chapel one can admire a precious wooden choir with 21 stalls, all carved, with carved panels on their backs, illustrating the articles of the Creed. It is one of the works of Domenico di Niccolò, who, having made this choir, was called « Domenico dei Cori ». This choir, made between 1415 and 1428, is a real masterpiece of woodworking art, thanks to its harmonious structure and elegant decorations.

« BALIA » HALL — This hall, divided into two sections by an arch, is so called after the College of the Judges of « Balia » (power), which used to hold its meetings in this very place. It is full of frescoes. The vaults, up to the cornices, were frescoed in 1407-1408 by the Sienese painter Martino di Bartolomeo, who divided the ceiling into triangular sections. In each section there is represented a Virtue. These Virtues are elegant feminine figures, which remind us of the painting of Ambrogio Lorenzetti. It is probably the best work of Martino di Bartolomeo. On the arch crossing the hall there are the figures of the Four Evangelists and six busts of emperors and warriors, while on the pillars there are other minor figures of Virtues. On the walls and lunettes above the arch there is a large cycle of frescoes made in 1408 by Spinello di Luca of Arezzo, called the Aretine (1346-1410). They represent the exploits of the pope Alexander III, belonging to the Sienese Bandinelli family, life and soul of the Lombard League and victor over Frederick Redbeard. This is one of the rare examples of the activity of a non-Sienese painter in Siena. Aretine, however, was well known in the town, because since 1404 he had been called by Sir Caterino di Corsino to paint in the Cathedral. These frescoes represent the last important work of this artist, who as helped by his son Parri, who was twenty at that time. They belong to the long 14th century tradition, dominated by the personality and activity of Giotto.

From the Balìa Hall, by a staircase, one can climb up to the large Loggia, open on four pillars, where the remains of Fonte Gaia, made by the Sienese Jacopo della Quercia, are kept. In the photo below, a corner of the hall; on the side plate, a detail of the oarsmen in « The naval battle between the Venetians and the Imperial forces at Punta Salvore », by Spinello Aretino.

BALIA HALL – Spinello Aretino – The entry of pope Alexander III in Rome and Alexander III gives his sword to the Doge of Venice. Though their forms are conventional because of the theme itself, the Stories of Alexander III present vivid narrative elements and are very interesting from the historical point of view, specially in the scenes illustrating the various events during the fight of the Pope against the Emperor Read-Beard. By these works the Aretine rises above the academic style, which was more interested in formal beauty than in the ideal message of art, and characterized most of the painting at the end of 14th century and the beginning of 15th century.

THE PILLARS HALL – The two precious partitions of predella representing « St. Bernardine preaching in a field », in the photo above, and « The miracolours deliverance of Genuzia from the devil during the funeral of St. Bernardine », were brought in the Palazzo Pubblico from the Gallery of the Academy during early 19th century. Now they are in the Pillars Hall which is in front of that of Peace. They were made by Neroccio di Bartolomeo Landi (1447-1500) and probably date back to the artist's young years. We do not know when the predella was made, but we get some indication from the first panel, where is represented the front of the Palazzo Pubblico with the Chapel, without the later additions made by Federeghi in 1468.

A sight of the back side of the Palazzo Pubblico with the Loggia and the Market Square. The latter one was so arranged in 1346 for the Market of animals, which once took place in the Campo. On the side page, another bautiful sight of the Tower of Mangia, with the old roofs of Siena and Cathedral: the dome, the bell-tower, and, on the left side, the « facciatone » (front) of what should have been the New Cathedral.

The Cathedral

The history of this building is long and complicate. Though it is one of the most known and magnificent cathedrals in Europe, we know little about the period and circumstances of its foundation. The first sure testimony dates back to 1136, when a special deputation of citizens was entrusted with the building of the Cathedral. Then it passed under the administration of the monks of San Galgano's Abbey, till 1314. In 1284 Giovanni Pisano built only the lower part of the facade. In the mean time the building was completed with its three aisles, dome and belfry. During the early 14th century, however, the Sienese, at the height of their prosperity and power, thought to erect a new magnificent building to be added perpendicularly to the south-east side of the cathedral. So the building of the New Cathedral began. Lando di Pietra was first entrusted with the works, then Giovanni d'Agostino. In 1348, however, because of a pestilence and the instability of the building, the works stopped and a few years later the project was put aside. The unsafe parts were demolished, while some of the perimetrical front walls, the left side aisle and the walls of the facade, the so called « facciatone » dominating the town, were left standing. So the building of the old Cathedral went on. In 1382 the apse was completed, the middle aisle was made higher and the upper part of the facade was erected by Giovanni di Cecco. Though various interruptions and time have left their signs in the planning structures and decorations of the Cathedral, this wonderful marble building presents an extraordinary unity, from the rich marble facade, with its splendid mosaics, to the more simple but elegant sides and pointed high tower with white and black strips and a series of mullioned windows. This unity is due to the original and wonderful balance between the Gothic elements, more evident on the outside, and Romanesque elements of the interior. The facade is one of the masterpieces of the Italian art. Its lower part, Romanesque, made by Giovanni Pisano, is characterized by three large portals and elegant statues made also by Pisano, here substituted with copies to prevent them to be damaged, while the originals are kept in the nearby museum. The upper part is of Gothic style, three-pointed and with a very rich decoration.

The column surmounted by the she-wolf and the elegant windows of the Archbishop's Palace, dating back to 18th century, to which the left part of the Cathedral was added. Below: a detail of the columns of the main door and the left side door of the facade of the Cathedral. In this front area one can admire a wonderful play of light and shade, thanks to the picturesque and abundant decoration of Pisano, made of small columns, carved jambs, corbels and cornices. It is an ideal space in which this great sculptor places his elegant figures, with their powerful lines and deep contrast of colours. It is an area of deep light, almost solidified by marble, a space suspended between earth and sky, made of matter and light, where the figures reach drama and purification at the same time.

The upper part of the main portal of the Cathedral, flanked with small columns adorned with a very beautiful classical decoration, wiht acanthus leaves, puttoes and animals, by Giovanni Pisano. In thc architrave there is a low-relief by Tino di Camaino (1285-1337), representing the « Story of St. Joachin and St. Anne ». The bronze door was made in 1958 by the sculptor Enrico Manfrini. It represents the Virgin glorified by God and men. Below: a detail of the left portal. Here, too, as in the right portal, there is a low-relief between the architrave and the arch. In the upper part of the facade, in the middle, there is a large rose-window with the Madonna and the four Evangelists, and, all around, busts of Patriarchs and prophets, all copies from originals dating back to 14th century and now kept in the nearby Museum. The three spires are covered with mosaics made by Aubusto Castellani (1877). The middle one is surmounted by an angel made by Tommaso Redi (1639).

LBERTI . D . FRANCISCI . DE . ARINGHERIIS . EQUITIS . HYEROSOLIMITAN .

INTERIOR — The Latin cross shaped interior of the Cathedral has three aisles.

It is austere and magnificent at the same time, with its play of light and shade on the marbles covering, with white and black stripes, walls and pillars. Here colour dominates. There is suggestive contrast between the vertical pillars and the horizontal decorative stripes. This gives special prominence to the Sienese picturesque fantasy and refined sense of colour. All along the nave runs a cornice, supported by 172 busts of popes, a work dating back to 15th-16th century. Below, there are the busts of 36 emperors. Along the side aisles and in the transepts there are splendid chapels, such as that of Our Lady of the Vow in the side transept and that of John the Baptist on the left side. In the elevated presbytery there is the main altar made by Baldassarre Peruzzi (1532). It is surmounted by a big bronze ciborium made by Vecchietta, put here in 1506 in the place of Duccio's « Maestà ». The marble floor, with its « graffito » and « tarsia » decorations, is one the masterpieces kept in this Cathedral. It consists of 56 tables representing biblical stories, sybils, virtues and various stories, made in different periods of time and by using different technics, from the second half of the 14th century to the middle of the 16th century. Out the more than 40 artists who took part in this work, we mention Matteo di Giovanni, who made « The Slaughter of the Innocents ». On a side, the Sybil Samia, by the same artist.

36

The Pulpit of Nicola Pisano

Near the hexagon of the dome there is the greatest masterpiece kept in the Cathedral, namely the Pulpit of Nicola di Maestro Pietro (1220-1284), called Nicola Pisano, since he stayed in that Tuscan town for a long time. Nicola is probably of Pugliese origin. He came in contact with the classical circles of the sculptores and architects of the time of Frederick II. Pisano, however, did not simply imitate the classics, but spontaneously assimilated the best aesthetic elements of the classical world. At the same time, he uses classical lines to express new and different ideas and values. And so, his art breaks with past tradition and begins a new one. The pulpit of Siena, one of the best works of the Italian sculpture, is an exceptional expression of this revival and artistic and human greatness of Pisano. It is made of white marble, octagonal, rests on nine columns, of which four have their bases with figures of lions and lionesses killing animals, four are without figures, and the middle one surrounded, below, by eight figures of the Arts. The parapet is adorned with seven reliefs representing stories of Christ from His birth to crucifixion and last judgement, and separated by statues of prophets and angels. In the pendentives of the trilobate arches there are other prophets and in the connections statues of virtues. This pulpit, sculptured between 1265 and 1268, was made a few years before the other one, also famous, of the Cathedral of Pisa, though it is stylistically more advanced than the latter. Instead of the aristocratic and detached figures of the pulpit of Pisa, its simple perspective and narrative solemnity, we have here a greater power of expression, a more free and complex plasticity, a more lively and dramatic partecipation of the characters in their deeds.

In the side photo we see a panel representing « The Nativity » and on the following plate, that of the ➤➤ « Last Judgement of the Good ».

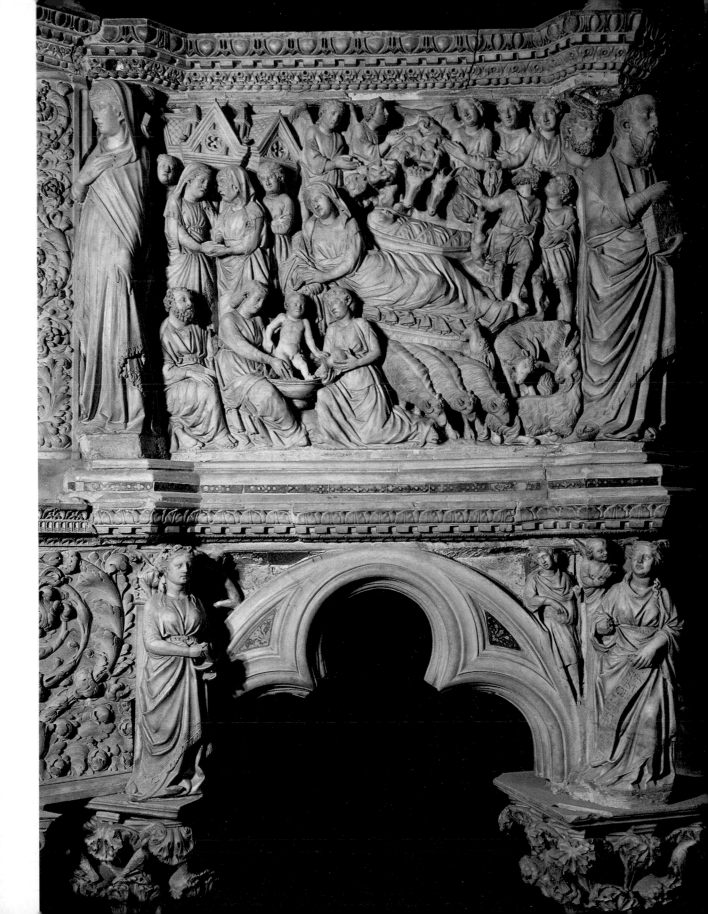

« The Adoration of the Magi » and « The Slaughter of the Innocents ». In these two panels we can see that, unlike the pulpit of Pisano, the figures are quite numerous, and the whole scene is much more animated and the faces are more expressive. Undoubtly here Gothic elements are present, but very strong is also the interpretation of the Roman sources, not only in the balance, but also in the dramatic severity of the story. It is perhaps the first time that in the Italian art human feelings are so expressed, without injuring the purity of a magnificent form.

«The Presentation of Jesus in the Temple », « The Flight into Egypt» and « The Last Judgement of the Reprobate ». The latter relief was probably made, together wiht that of the « Slaughter of the Innocents, by Giovanni, son of Nicola Pisano. The Judgement dominates the scene: it occupies two sides with the figure of Christ in the centre, separating the Good from the Reprobate. The second scene, that of the Reprobate, is the most impressive and dramatic one. Apart from Giovanni Pisano, Arnolfo di Campio took part in this work. The stylistic homogeneity of this work, however, shows the maturity and greatness of the artistic personality of Nicola, who was conscious of the intrinsic historicity of culture.

In the photos above, we see the details of the base of the main column of the pulpit, surrounded by eight figures representing the Seven Liberal Arts and Music; below, the details of the « Flight into Egypt » and the « Crucifixion ». On the right plate, the wonderful panel of the « Crucifixion », a very realistic and dramatic scene. For the first time in the history of sculpture, Christ is a presented by Nicola Pisano as magnificently human, since the sacred history is where human and divine spheres meet.

The main altar (see photo above) is adorned with the big bronze ciborium made by Vecchietta, and four angels bearing chandeliers, of which two made by Giovanni di Stefano (1489) and two, together with the half figures of angels, are masterpieces of Francesco di Giorgio Martini (1497-99). On the pillars, on bronze corbels, there are eight angels made by Domenico Beccafumi (1548-1550), of which one can be seen in the photo above, on the right side. On a side we can admire a detail of the bronze statue of John the Baptist, by Donatello, placed in the chapel of St. John the Baptist. It was made in Florence and sent to Siena in the October of 1457. It expresses a tormented spirituality and a deep asceticism. This statue date back to the last active years of the Master and was made a little the Repentant Magdalen of the Baptistery of Florence, which it resembles in its style and spirituality.

46

In the apse there is the magnificent wooden choir, which occupies the lower part of the niche for the whole lenght of the three aisles. It was begun in 1363 and finished in 1397. Originally it consisted of more than 90 stalls in a double line, surmounted by canopies and adorned by tabernacles and statues of saints. The part on the sides of the niche is all that remains of the wonderful 14th century work with carvings made by Francesco and Jacopo del Tonghio. The splendid marbles on the back of the stalls were made by Fra' Giovanni of Verona. They were made for the choir of St. Benedict's Convent at Porta Tufi and later placed in the choir of the Cathedral in 1503. They reproduce beautiful still lives and sights of towns. The magnificent middle stalls, in the Renaissance style, were carved by Teseo Bartolini of Pienza and Benedetto di Giovanni of Montepulciano, on design of Riccio, in the second half of the 16th century. The choir, on the whole, is a very refined and magnificent work.

THE DOME — The hexagonal shaped dome was built between 1259 and 1264.
It is supported by six pillars. In each of its corners there are big golden statues of saints, by Ventura Tiparilli and Bastiano di Francesco, resting on columns. Above, some shell-shaped niches change the hexagon into a dodecagon, in which there is a gallery divided by 42 small columns with figures of patriarchs and prophets. The figures were painted in 1481 by Guidoccio Cozzarelli, Benvenuto di Giovanni and Pellegrino di Mariano. Above the gallery there are the asymmetrical cap of the dome and the lantern restored in 1891. This hexagonal dome is very suggestive thanks to its perspective effects. Below it, the floor keeps, within hexagons and rhombs, many biblical stories attributed to Domenico Beccafumi (1486-1551), the most famous Sienese painter in the 16th century. The stories were remade by Alessandro Franchi.
On the outside, the dome is covered by robust ribs and rests on a drum formed by two orders of galleries. The lower one is enclosed by ogive arches supported by double columns, and the upper one has round arches. When in 1376 the building of the New Cathedral stopped and Giovanni Cecco began to complete the facade, they wanted to make it higher and more imposing. So the building had to be raised and the lower order of the small porticoes of the dome was completely smothered.

PICCOLOMINI ALTAR – The majestic altar, which is along the left aisle, was made by order of Cardinal Francesco Piccolomini in 1481. It is one of Andrea Bregno's works. The Madonna, in the niche above: it attributed to Jacopo della Quercia, while the delicate Madonna with the Child, placed in the marble altarpiece is attributed to Paolo di Giovanni Fei (1381). The statues, made by Michelangelo and placed in the niches, are very interesting: Sts. Paul and Peters langelo and placed in the niches, are very interesting: Sts. Paul and Peter Piccolomini had ordered fifteen of them, but the great artist made only four, between 1501 and 1504. These are among the less known works of Michelangelo, though they are of a very high artistic value.

Piccolomini Library

In the first span of the left aisle there is the Piccolomini Library. Its building began in 1492 by order of Cardinal Francesco Piccolomini Todeschini, the future Pope Pius III, to collect here the books of the library of Pope Pius II, his uncle on his mother's side. The marble front has elegant decorations by Marrina and is surmounted by a fresco by Bernardino di Betto, named the Pinturicchio (1454-1513), with the Coronation of Pius III.

In the interior of the library, formed by only one rectangular hall, one is struck by its vivid and beautiful colours. In the centre of the hall, on a Renaissance base, there is the group of the «Three Graces» a copy of a Hellenistic original dating back to the III century. This work was donated by Cardinal Piccolomini to be placed in the library. Along the walls, enclosed in pendentives and strips, there are the frescoes made by Pinturicchio between 1505 and 1508. They tell episodes of the life of Enea Silvio Piccolomini, born in Corsignano (Pienza) in 1405, archbishop of Siena, then pope from 1458 to 1464, a famous humanist, diplomat and pontif. This work, however, does not show the freshness and high spirituality of the frescoes in the Baglioni Chapel of Spello or the Borgia's Rooms in the Vatican. Yet these stories strike us with their vivid colours, simple and lively narration, without dramatic emphasis, the illustrative capacities of Pinturicchio, a magnificent decorator.

Four of the 10 scenes of the Life of Pius II: from left above: Enea Silvio Piccolomini receives the cardinal's hat from Pope Callisto III; Enea Silvio Piccolomini made Pope with the name of Pius II; Pius II canonizes St. Catherine of Siena; Pius II in Mantova to promote the crusade against the Turks. ➤

PICCOLOMINI LIBRARY – Miniated choir-books. In the interior of the library, on benches carved by Antonio Barili in 1496, there are the wonderful choir-books miniated by Liberale of Verona (1445ca-1529) and Girolamo of Cremona (first half of the 15th century). It is a very refined work, which the best example of the miniature art in 15th century Italy. During the previous centuries miniature had much developed mainly in North Italy, where it had put aside the Byzantine models and followed the great Franch-Gothic tradition. In the 13th century the miniature production in Bologna and Emilia was remarkable for quality and quantity. These artists were specialized in illustrating civil and canon law books used in the University. And it was the Bolognese School that influenced the production in central Italy, where it was less rich and interesting, though there were works of great value and originality. Two centuries later, the great masters of the North are still the leaders in the miniature art. And it was in Siena, where they stayed in the second half of the 15th century that Liberale and Girolamo miniated their masterpierces, namely a series of choir-books for the sacristy of the Cathedral. Today they are kept in the Piccolomini library. Together with the choir-books made by these two masters, educated in the Paduan atmosphere of Mantegna's times, whose stay in the Tuscan town influenced the Sienese painting at the end of the 15th century, there are others made by Sienese artists, such as Sano di Pietro, Pellegrino di Mariano and Guidoccio Cozzarelli.

On the side page we can admire the ceiling of the library, frescoed by Pinturicchio in 1502-1503 and divided into panels with mythological and allegorical themes. In the middle, surrounded by a garland of fruits, there is the coat-of-arms of Piccolomini family.

The Museum of the Cathedral

The Museum of the Cathedral is situated in the first three arcades of the right aisle of the New Cathedral. It was constituted in 1870 and later renewed many times. It includes mainly works of art created to embellish the Cathedral and later transferred into the Museum to preserve them or because they were removed from their places and replaced with other works during the restorations in the 16th and 17th centuries. The collection includes sculptural and pictorial groups, bronzes, wooden and terra-cotta objects, gold ware, embroideries and miniature, all works of great artistic value, thanks to which this is one of the richest and most important museums in Italy. In it one finds some famous masterpieces of the Sienese and Tuscan art from the 13th to the 14th century, made by Simon Martini, Pietro Lorenzetti and Jacopo della Quercia, apart from the statues made by Giovanni Pisano for the facade of the Cathedral and the « Maestà » by Duccio di Buoninsegna, all works of incomparable beauty, which are the pride of Siena and some of the greatest artistic expressions in the whole world. On the ground floor, in a hall divided into two sections by a large wrought iron railing dating back to the 14th century, there are, among many other works, fragments of architectonic elements and sculptures of the facade and the interior of the Cathedral; marble plutei of Pisano's school; a front of a Roman sarcophagus dating back to the imperial age; a splendid high-relief dating back to the late maturity of Jacopo della Quercia. Along the walls there are the ten statues sculptured by Giovanni Pisano and removed from the facade of the Cathedral since the second half of the last century. On the first floor there is Duccio's Hall, so called because there is the magnifcent and famous « Maestà ». Here we can admire also the « Nativity of the Virgin » by Pietro Lorenzetti and the « Madonna of Crevole », a work of the young Duccio, coming from St. Cecily's church at Crevole. On the second floor, there is the Treasure Hall, where are kept the most precious sacred furniture of the Cathedral, among which a reliquary of the head of St. Galgano (13th century), a small wooden crucifix of Giovanni Pisano and the wooden busts of the saints Crescentius, Savinus and Victor, made by Francesco di Vandambrino (1409). On the last floor, there is a picture-gallery and the so called « Saloncino dei Conversari », with works of Ambrogio Lorenzetti, Matteo di Giovanni, Sodoma, Domenico Beccafumi. Through a small door of this hall, a few steps lead to the top of the « Facciatone », from where one can enjoy a wonderful view

This is the larger lower Hall of the Museum, where are kept the Winged Bull and Lion by Giovanni Pisano, apart from some original fragments of the floor of the Cathedral. At the entrance, after the railing, there is the She-wolf with the Twins, also a work of Pisano and emblem of Siena, and the original work, of which that on the column near the Cathedral is a copy.

In the centre of the hall, on the ground floor, there is, as we have said, the high-relief made by Jacopo della Quercia, representing « The Madonna with the Child, St. Anthony the Abbot and Cardinal Antonio Casini kneeling ». This work, once lost and recently found, dates back to the last period of Jacopo's activity. It is plastically powerful and deeply moral and this fact shows how the artist, in his sculptures, at times resembles Donatello. If, on one side, the rich drapery and a subtle psychologism still connect Jacopo della Quercia with the traditional culture, on the other, the presence of drama, seen as history of which man is the protagonist, is a sign of his partecipation and a consciously humanistic atmosphere.

MARY OF MOSES – It is perhaps the most beautiful of the ten statues made for the facade of the Cathedral by Giovanni Pisano, born between 1240 and 1245 and educated under shelter of his father's art. However, he went for his own way, rejecting the Hellenic serenity of Nicola and preferring the transalpine Gothic sculpture to it.

ABACUC – These statues, among which the pathetic Abacuc, were made between 1285 and 1296. They represent biblical figures, ancient philosophers and prophets, taller than usual. They constitute one of the most important and daring work of the Gothic and European sculptural art and a masterpiece of Giovanni Pisano.

MOSES, SIBYL, ISAIAH — These graceful figures, with that spiral drapery and the brusque movement with their heads, show an extraordinary vitality, which overcomes matter and expresses itself mainly in the faces with their well-defined features. Here we find the whole world of Pisano — a dramatic and, at times, tormented world, where he combines plastic forms with feelings on a plane we could call expressionistic. Placing himself between the classicism of his father's art and the Gothic of the transalpine and specially French art, he reaches the height of his poetical research, trying to create an impetuous and dramatic vision.

The "Maestà,, of Duccio

The magnificent « Maestà » is praised by the chroniclers of that time, who describe the parade by which this work was taken into the church by the people and local authorities. It is the masterpiece of Duccio di Buoninsegna (1278-1318), the first great Sienese artist, who knew how to change various elements into poetical themes by combining the aulic preciosity of the Byzantine patterns with the human lyricism of the French Gothic style. With the « Maestà » the 13th century pictorical experience comes to an end and a new age begins. The great development of the 14th century Sienese school is mainly due to him. The monumental painting, ordered on October 9, 1308 and completed after about three years, had to adorn the main alter of the Cathedral, where it was placed on June 9, 1311, but it was removed two centuries later. Then it was dismembered and transferred in 1876 into the Museum of the Cathedral. On its front there is the Madonna with the Child among worshiping angels and saints. On the back, in front of the « Maestà », divided into 26 parts, are represented episodes of the Passion of Christ, separated by a large middle strip which marks a break between the first scenes, in the lower order, and the last ones, in the upper order. Once this work had a predella with Stories of Christ's Childhood (seven on the front) and His Public life (ten on the back), and a Gothic gable including 16 panels with episodes of the Life of the Madonna(on the front) and the Risen Christ (on the back). Out of these latter parts, five panels got lost, while some others are now kept in museums and foreign collections; others, 19 panels, are kept in the Museum together with the front and the back of the work.

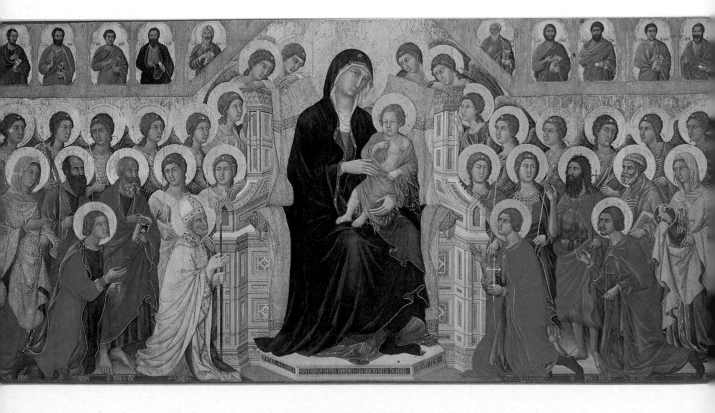

DETAILS OF THE « MAESTA' » – The four Patron Saints of Siena. St. Crescentinus, St. Savinus, St. Ansanus and St. Victor are presented on the forreground, while worshiping. On the side plate, the figure of t. Agnes: it is a very graceful image vibrating with deep feelings.

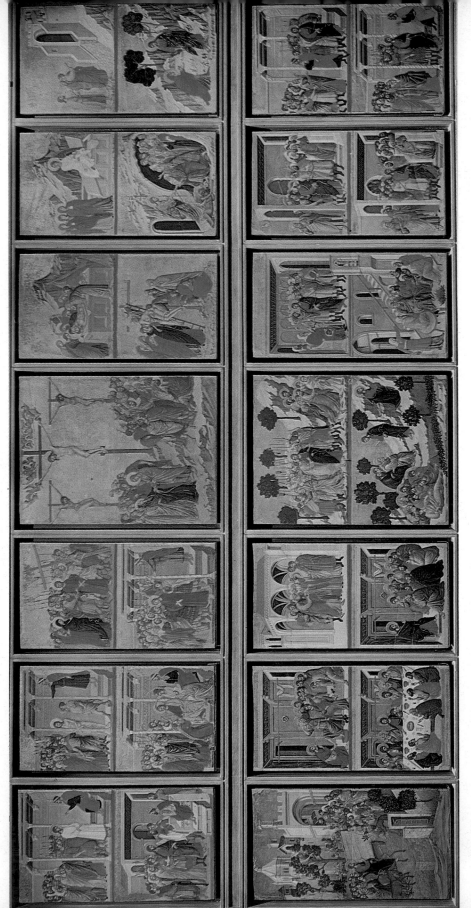

Here we can admire the 26 panels of the back, representing the Stories of the Passions of Christ, from the Entry in Jerusalem to the Apparitions at Emmaus, where a new and different harmony is created by the play of colours and lines, in a constant and various rythm, including each scene and the scenes of the whole cycle. In the middle, the panel of the Crucifixion, larger than the others, and tragically beautiful. On a golden background, above a crowd of various people, the Christ divides the scene in a dramatic crescendo, where Duccio's art reaches the height of poetry.

The 26 panels – From above and from left to right:

1/2 - Christ sent to Pilate and Christ before Herod. 3/4 - The Scourging and Crowning with Thorns. 5/6 - Going up to Calvary and Pilate washing his hand. 7 - The Crucifixion. 8/9 - Christ taken down from the cross and buried. 10/11 - Mary at the Tomb and the Descent into the Limbus. 12/13 - Apparition at Emmaus and « Noli me tangere » (Do not touch me).

Lower panels

14 - Jesus entering Jerusalem. 15/16 - Jesus washing His disciples' feet and the Last Supper. 17/18 - Judas' Pact and Christ's Farewell. 19/20 - Judas' kiss and Prayer in the Garden. 21/22 - Christ before Annah and Peter's Denial. 23/24 - Christ beaten and Christ before Caiphah. 25/26 - Christ accused by the Pharisees and Christ before Pilate.

MAESTA' – Details of the back: Christ Beaten and Christ before Caiphah, Christ accused by the Pharisees and Christ before Pilate, in the panel above; Christ washing His disciples' feet and the Last Supper, Judas' Pact and Christ's Farewell, in the panel below. On the side plate: Judas' Kiss and the Prayer in the Garden. It is in these small panels that Duccio's language creates his masterpieces. It is here that his art becomes now lyric and then rational, narrative and pathetic. His use of colour, a very refined design, the great formal harmony based on the combination of colours and lines, together with the experience of the miniature art and the Gothic-French sculpture give him the possibility of raising the declined old figurative culture to the height of art and poetry.

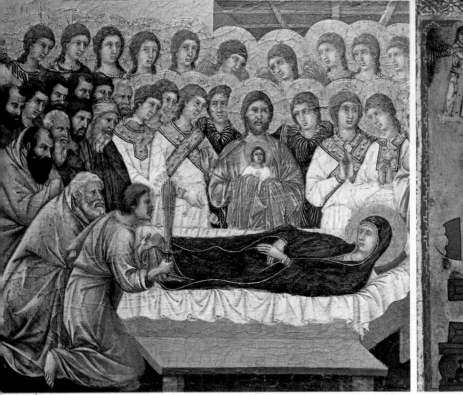

In the first hall of the picture-gallery situated on the third floor of the Museum, among some interesting works of the Sienese school, there is the so called « Madonna with large eyes », dating back to the beginning of the 13th century. It is one of the oldest works of the Sienese painting art. Once it was on the main altar of the Cathedral, before the Maestà was placed there. The people of Siena knelt before it, before the battle of Monteaperti, which took place in 1260.

In the other two photos are represented the panels of the Coronation of the « Maestà », with the Deaht of Mary and the Funeral of Mary. Duccio was able to express the deep and poetical meanings of each episode.

THE NATIVITY OF MARY – Pietro Lorenzetti – (Detail). It is situated in the Hall of the Maestà. It is the last known work of Lorenzetti (1280 ca - 1348), who, among the early 13th century masters, follows Giotto more closely. Here the artist, putting aside the traditional division of the polyptics, has represented only one scene in the right panel and in the middle one, with a new perspective and greater narrative vivacity.

The Baptistery

The Baptistery, called also « Pieve di San Giovanni », rises on the back of the Cathedral and is the base of the continuation of its head, like a crypt. Its facade, begun in 1317 and again in 1382, erroneously attributed to Giacomo di Mino del Pelicciaio, was probably made by Domenico d'Agostino. It shows a true decorative preciosity. Incomplete in its upper part, it is mostly made of white marble and consists of three large portals flanked with small columns and marble decorations. In the middle there are pensile arches and, above, blind ogive windows. On the floor, before the portals, there are marble graffitoes representing the Sacraments of Baptism and Confirmation; that before the left door, representing the « Birth of Man » with a woman in labour and a new-born baby, is one of the works of Bartolomeo di Mariano, called « Mandriano » (1450). The other two, with the scene of the Baptism before the main door and Confirmation before the right portal, were made by Antonio Federighi (1451). The interior of the Baptistery is vast and luminous. It was completed in 1325 under the direction of Camaino di Crescentino. It is rectangular and divided into three aisles. Its vaults, apse and two lunettes above the side altars are completely covered with frescoes. Those made by Lorenzo di Pietro, called Vecchietta (1447-1450) are very precious. They occupy the vaults where are represented the Articles of the Creed, the Prophets and the Sybils, and the walls of the apse with two scenes of the life of Christ, the « Scourging » and « Going to Calvary ». The other paintings were made by Michele di Matteo of Bologna and Benvenuto di Giovanni (late 15th century).

THE FONT, erected on two steps in the centre of the church, has, at its base, a hexagonal basin and, above, a pillar supporting a hexagonal ciborium. The ciborium, designed by Jacopo della Quercia, is surmonted by a small column on which rests a beautiful statue of the Baptist, made by Jacopo. The small well, made from 1417 on by Sano di Matteo, Nanni di Jacopo of Lucca and Jacopo di Corso of Florence, on design erroneously attributed to Jacopo della Quercia, has six lcw-reliefs in golden bronze, which extol the life of St. John the Baptist. On the plate we see one of the low-reliefe made by Lorenzetti Ghiberti (1378-1455), who made also the famous « Gates of Heaven » of the Florence Baptistery. Here is represented the « Arrest of the a Baptist », a very refined work, very elegant in its forms and serene plasticity.

Here we can at last admire the magnificent Font. The reliefs around the small well begin, on the side towards the altar, with « The Angel announcing Baptist's Birth to Zechariah », by Jacopo della Quercia (1428-29) and go on with the « Baptist's Birth » and the «Baptist's Preaching», by Giovanni di Turino (1427), the « Baptism of Christ » and the « Arrest of the Baptist », by Lorenzo Ghiberti (1427) and « Herod's Banquet » by Donatello (1427). With the six low-reliefs alternate some statues made by Donatello, « Faith » and « Hope », by Giovanni di Turino, « Justice », « Charity » and « Providence », and by Goro di Ser Neroccio, « Fortitude ». The statues of prophets adorning the ciborium in the niches, were made by Jacopo della Quercia, while Turino made the delicate Madonna with the Child on the door. Donatello and Giovanni di Turino made also the bronze angels on the front of the tabernacle. Many artists took part in the building of the Font. In spite of this, it is stylistically uniform and can be considered a true masterpiece of the plastic and scultural art.

BAPTISMAL FONT
« The Baptism of Jesus »
by Lorenzo Ghiberti;
« The Angel announces
to Zechariah the Baptist's Birth », by Jacopo
della Quercia, and « Herod's Banquet » by Donatello.

BAPTISMAL FONT
« The Baptist's Birth »
and « The Preaching of
the Baptist », both made
by Giovanni di Turino.

76

BAPTISMAL FONT – «Hope» by Donatello: together with the « Faith » is one of the first statues made by this artist. It expresses a deep spirituality and is the personification of the soul's elevation to God.

77

BAPTISMAL FONT – « Justice », by Giovanni di Turino (1424).

BAPTISMAL FONT – « Fortitude », by Goro di Ser Neroccio (1428).

THE BAPTISTERY – « Jesus climbing Calvary » (a detail), by Vecchietta, who made most of the frescoes of the church. In the apse, on the opposite wall, there is the « Scourging of Christ at Pilate's court », a highly dramatic work, in which the artist, by those suffering and tense faces, expresses his partecipation in the drama.

THE MADONNA OF THE PROPHETS – This 19th century triptych, by Giuseppe Catano, adorns the right side altar of the Baptistery. Above the left one, there are the frescoes represenitng « St. Anthony Miracles », made by Benvenuto di Giovanni, perhaps on design of Vecchietta.

The National Picture-Gallery

The National Picture-Gallery of Siena is situated in Palazzo Buonsignori, one of the most elegant late-Gothic buildings of the town. It includes a collection of works which are very important for the knowledge of the sienese painting art from the end of the 12th century to the first half of the 17th century. Its origin dates back to the 18th century, when the abbot Giuseppe Ciaccheri collected some paintings to donate them to the town of Siena. Later on, works coming from various donations, store-rooms, churches, convents, religious and lay associations, which had been suppressed, enriched the collection. It was housed, first, in the Institute of Fine Arts, later, in 1930, in Palazzo Buonsignori, under the State Administration, The Picture Gallery keeps about 700 paintings arranged in 28 halls according tho chronological order or various styles. The greatest masters and less known painters are present here with some of their works. Works which are masterpieces known all over the world, are exhibited together with less important works. All of them, however, contribute to form an incomparably valuable patrimony and the most peculiar testimony of the painting school of Siena, which was, as Roberto Paribeni said, « the perfect image of a world, happy and gentle synthesis of the great spiritual riches of Italy ». Below, is represented the facade of Palazzo Buonsignori, built after 1440 by Giovanni di Guccio Bichi, a very rich Sienese banker, and a few years later sold to Tegliacci brothers. In 1476 it was bought by the Buonsignori family, whose last descendant donated it to the town to be used as a museum. The brick facade, with a stone base is one of the last examples of Gothic architecture. Below it has some blind arches, and on the first and second floors there are elegant three-mullioned windows divided by a cornice of pensile arches. Among the merlons of the crowning there are marble panels with stucco heads.

MADONNA OF THE FRANCISCANS — It dates back around 1300. It is one of the most renowned works ➤ of Duccio di Boninsegna. His art, though grounded in the ancient Byzantine tradition, shows a very refined and pathetically human emphasis.

THE ADORATION OF THE MAGI – It is probably the masterpiece of Bartolo di Fredi and was made between 1370 and 1380. It is a very fine work, thanks to its rich details, vivid colours; the ANNUNCIATION, a very fine and lyric work of Francesco di Giorgio Martini, one of the most complex and charming artistic personalities in the late 15th century. On a side: POLYPTYC OF ST. DOROTHY, by Ambrogio Lorenzetti. This work, made around 1332, represents the Madonna with the Child, St. Mary Magdalen in the left panel and St. Dorothy in the right one.

The small «MAESTA'», on the right side, is another very fine work of Ambrogio Lorenzetti who made it around 1340. It is very important because of its perspecitve anticipations and great solemnity.

CHRIST AT THE PILLAR, by Giovanni Antonio Bazzi, called SODOMA (1477-1549). It is a spiritually and stilistically refined work, which was a part of a greater work made between 1511 and 1514 for the convent of St. Francis in Siena.

THE ADORATION OF THE SHEPHERDS, by Taddeo di Bartolo (1362-1422), dating back to the end of the 14th century, a very sober and genuine work.

A TOWN ON THE SEA, by Ambrogio Lorenzetti. This small painting and the other one on the side page, come from the Archives of the Municipality and probably represent places of the ancient State of Siena. This town on the sea is probably Talamone, a port of the Republic. Thanks to its delicate colours and clear forms, the two paintings constitute some of the finest works kept in the Picture-Gallery. In them reality is transformed into a magically charming atmosphere. They are very interesting not only because of their artistic value, but also because they are the first paintings of the European art, which represent landscapes.

THE FLIGHT TO EGYPT – Together with two other paintings, THE PRESENTATION OF MARY IN THE TEMPLE and THE CRUCIFIXION, this work is a part of a predella, made in 1436 by Giovanni di Paolo (1399-1482). This artist's poetry goes beyond reality and gets into a trascendent sphere.

THE ROLY FAMILY WITH ST. JOHN AS A CHILD, by Pinturicchio. It dates back to the late years of this artist, who stayed in Siena for a long time to fresco the vaults of the Piccolomini Library. This work, coming from the Convent of Campansi, shows all the characteristics of the Umbrian painter, who was an elegant and magnificent decorator.

CASTLE ON THE BANKS OF A LAKE, by Ambrogio Lorenzetti is not a disciple of Pietro, his elder brother, but follows, Cimabue, Giotto and Simone Martini. He follows these great artists through the minor personalities who constitute the environment of that time. In the case of this fine painting, the artist was probably inspired by a garrison of the Sienese Republic, situated on the lake of Chiusi or on the Trasimeno.

While we see towers and embattled walls all crowded in the centre of the preceding painting, here we have a country landscape, which in an atmosphere of quiet and solitude, shows a deep and charming lyricism.

THE ANNUNCIATION, by Ambrogio Lorenzetti. This work is signed and dated 1344. It is the last known work of the great painter. In it we note the particularly well chosen colours, its rich decorations, a new perspective, together with a conscious serenity by which the Mistery is interpreted.

PORTRAIT OF ELISABETH QUEEN OF ENGLAND, attributed to Federico Zuccari (1542-1606). In the same hall there are works of G. B. Moroni, Scarsellino, Bernardo Strozzi and Padovanino, all painters of the 17th and 18th centuries.

THE NATIVITY, by Andrea di Bartolo (1389-1428), a Sienese painter, son of Bartolo di Fredi, whose disciple and co-operator he was. His style, though influenced by his father's, shows a greater freedom as regards composition and chromatic vividness.

MADONNA ON A THRONE, a detail of the Ancona of Carmel, painted by Pietro Lorenzetti in 1328-1329 for the Church of Carmel in Siena. The great ancona dismembered in 1500, included a central panel with the Madonna on a throne, with St. Nicholas of Bari and the Prophet Elijah on her sides, and a predella with five panels, in which are represented the foundation and the first events of the Carmelite Order. The great statuesque plasticity, the severe harmony of the few dominating colours and a dynamic tension of its lines, make of this work one of the masterpieces of the artist's mautrity.

THE MADONNA APPEARS TO CAL-LISTUS IIII (1456), by Sano di Pie-tro (1406-1481). Apart from this painting, this artist's production is largely present in other three halls of the Picture-Gallery.

ST. JEROME IN THE DESERT — It belongs to a triptych made in 1436, whose upper part is now in the Basilica of the Observance near Siena. For a long time it was at-tributed to Sassetta. Today it is thought to be the work of an artist who painted in a style similar to that of Salsetta and called the « Master of the Observance ».

THE LAST SUPPER, by Stefano di Giovanni called Sassetta (about 1392-1450). This painting was a part of an ancona made between 1423 and 1426 for the Chapel of the Wool-workers' Guild of Siena. It is the first work of Sassetta, and very important for the history of the Sienese painting art in the 15th century. In it we perceive the influence of Simone Martini and Pietro Lorenzetti, but their styles are re-interpreted in a new and modern manner. Its colour is intensely luminous and transparent.

MADONNA WITH THE CHILD (a detail), by Matteo di Giovanni (1430-1495), a remarkable work for its pure and simple lines.

LUCRECE, of the school of Luke Cranach (1472-1553), a German painter who made many portraits and kept an active workshop at the service of various princely courst of Germany. In the same hall there are works of other Fleminsh and German masters.

89

OUR LADY OF SOR-
ROWS, by Ugolino di
Nerio, a Sienese painter
of the first half of the
XVth century. In his art,
he follows Duccio and
the Lorenzetti's circle.

THE MYSTICAL MAR-
RIAGE OF ST. CATHE-
RINE OF ALEXANDRIA,
by Michelino of Besozzo
(of whom we have in-
formations from 1388 to
1442). This painter was
very important as far as
the international paint-
ing art in Lombardia is
concerned. The painting
here exhibited is a par-
ticular example of his
over-refined decorative
art.

THE NATIVITY OF JESUS, by Pietro di Domenico (1457-1503). This delicate work, with its beautiful details, is the only one signed by the artist, who was very active in the Marche, treading on the wake of Gentile of Fabbriano and the Umbrian painters, mainly Pinturicchio.

MADONNA WITH THE CHILD, ST. JOHN THE BAPTIST AND ST. ANDREW, by Neroccio di Bartolomeo Landi (1447-1500). As a painter and sculptor, a disciple of Vecchietta, he represents, with his work, the epilogue of the Sienese figurative culture. He expresses in the painting, rather than in sculpture, its delicate sensitivity for design.

POPE HONORIUS APPROVES THE CARMELITE RULE — It is one of the panels of the great painting of Piero Lorenzetti. In this short stories, Lorenzetti's language becomes solemn in its chromatic forms and the influence of Martin'is colour effects and his brother Ambrose, an attentive observer, is quite evident. Here this artist reaches heights of magic beauty and poetry, even when describing the humblest sides of everyday life. Of a very high quality are also the two panels representing the « DREAM OF SEBACH, FATHER OF THE PROPHET ELIJAH » and the « FIRST CARMELITE HERMITS AT ELIJAH'S FOUNT ».

By night Siena is immersed in a peculiar and charming atmosphere, which the tourist perceive when admiring the noble elegance of the Palazzo Pubblico and the solemn magnificence of the Cathedral, or walking along the old and picturesque alleys climbing up among houses leaning one against the other, among vaults and buttresses. It is a town with a magic scenography, which seems to have come out of a fairy-story book.

ST. JOSEPH'S ARCH AND FOUNTAIN of the Contrada of the Wave. Each contrada has a small fountain placed along the main street or near the Oratory and bearing a small statue representing the emblem of the contrada. On the feast of the Patron Saint the children born during the year are baptized with the water springing from these fountains.

◄ CHURCH OF HOLY MARY OF THE SERVANTS – This church was built in the 13th century and later enlarged. It rises on the top of a high flight of steps, on a solitary square with trees. The simple and austere facade has only one portal surmounted by two rose-windows, while the Romanesque belfry with one-mullioned windows which in the upper part become four-mullioned windows. The interior, with Renaissance aisles and Gothic transept and apse, keeps precious works of art.

St. Bernardine's Oratory

St. Bernardine's Oratory is on the right side of St. Francis' Square, where the basilica of St. Francis rises. This church was built in 1326 on the place of a pre-existing small church and later many times modified. Its interior is very interesting for its architectonic structure and frescoes. The nearby old Convent of St. Francis, recently restored, houses the Faculty of Economical and Banking Sciences of the University.

The Oratory consists of two superimposed orders, the lower oratory and the upper oratory. It was built in the 15th century on the place where St. Bernardine used to pray. Bernardine was born in Massa Marittima in 1380 and died in L'Aquila in 1444. He devoted himself to humanistic and law studies, till he joined the Franciscan Order, when he was 22. He began his preaching ministery in Genova, and travelled all over Northern and Central Italy. He distinguished himself for his genuineness. Bernardine was a providential reformer for the Franciscan Order and for the Catholic world the promoter of a new spiritual zeal, which influenced the religious and civil life of his times.

In the photo we can admire the interesting upper oratory, with ceiling and wooden walls stuccoed by Ventura Turapilli in 1496. Among the pillars there are very precious frescoes made by Sodoma, Girolamo del Pacchia and Domenico Beccafumi. « St. Francis of Assisi » by Sodoma, is perhaps the most beatiful of these frescoes. The lower oratory is decorated by 17th century paintings: a « Madonna with the Child and Sts. Bartholomew and Ansanus » by Andrea del Brescianino is placed near the altar, on whose sides there are two niches with the statues of St. Bernardine and St. Catherine, painted in white, dating back to the 17th century. Near the altar there are some precious works, such as a « Madonna with the Child » in painted wood of the school of Jacopo della Quercia, a « Madonna » by Sano di Pietro and a very delicate low-relief made by Giovanni d'Agostino.

ORATORY – « Presentation of Mary in the Temple », by Sodoma. This was one of the greatest Piedmontese painters of Renaissance, who worked mainly in Siena, where he had moved when he was very young.

ORATORY – « The Marriage of Mary », by Domenico Beccafumi (1486-1551). He was the last one of the great Sienese painters and one of the most famous representatives of Mannerism. This current began towards the middle of the 16th century and inclined to a precious unreality by the attractive possibilities of colour and light.

ORATORY — « Madonna with the Child » by Sano di Pietro. The artist presents here once again his ideal image of the Virgin by using very delicate lines.

ORATORY — « The Coronation of Mary », by Sodoma, of which we can admire a detail and the whole work. The painting is in front of the altar, where are kept the relic of St. Bernardine's heart and the tablet with Jesus' monogram, used by Bernardine.

101

Basilica of St. Dominic

The imposing basilica of St. Dominic dominates the hill, at whose foot there is Fonte Branda, the most beautiful and famous of the many Sienese fortified fountains. This work, in a severe Gothic style and all in bricks, was begun in 126 by the Dominicans who built the rectangular nave and the open truss ceiling. Around 1300 they built the crypt which, being so large, is practically a church, so much so that it was called the Lower Church or Church of the Dead, because it housed some tombs. It was restored in 1935. It consists of one large room with three aisles and keeps works of Sodoma, Ventura Salimbeni, Sano di Pietro and Turino di Sano. The belfry was built in 1340 and in the 14th century the building of the basilica went on and was completed in 1465. It was severely damaged by fire in 1532 and earthquake in 1779. Later it was restored and today it has its original structure. The Egyptian cross-shaped interior has only one nave and is very simple and imposing. The chapel of St. Catherine, on the right wall, is very interesting. In it there are frescoes made by Sodoma, and considered to be some of his masterpieces, such as « St. Catherine's Ecstasy and Fainting Fit », and the chapel of the vaults, which keeps, near the altar, a painting of Andrea Vanni, representing St. Catherine of Siena, considered to be the only true portrait of Catherine Benincasa. Together with other important works of art, particularly noteworthy are the ciborium and two marble angels near the main altar of the basilica, made by Benedetto da Maiano around 1475, two beautiful paintings of Matteo di Giovanni (1479) and a fresco by Pietro Lorenzetti. From the right side of the facade one gets into the cloister of St. Dominic, built in 1425, almost completely remade in 1951, where some fragments of frescoes made by Lippo Memmi and Andrea Vanni (14th century) have been found.

BASILICA OF ST. DOMINIC

The elegant square belfry made of bricks, quite modified during the 18th century, and the incomplete facade. On its left side there were the niches in which some aristocratic tombs were placed. Below: the fresco representing st. Catherine portrait made by Andrea Vanni, a disciple of hers, and on the right side: « St. Barbara on a throne among angels and Sts. Magdalen and Catherine »; in the lunette, « Epiphany », a masterpiece of Matteo di Giovanni, made in 1479. The painting is in the second chapel of the left transpet.

On the plate of the next page, a partial view of Siena seen from the church of St. Dominic, dominated by the Tower of Mangia and the imposing building of the Cathedral and its belfry. ➤

ST. CATHERINE'S CHAPEL —
Near the altar there is a
marble tabernacle, made by
Giovanni di Stefano in 1466,
containing Catherine's head.
The chapel was almost completely frescoed by Sodoma,
of whom we see on the left
side: « The saint interced-
ing for the execution of Niccolò
di Tuldo », and on the right:
« St. Catherine's fainting fit ».
They are very valuable paintings specially for the figure
of Catherine and the harmony
of the group.
On a side: « The saint deli-
vering a possessed person »,
an oil-painting on wall, by
Francesco Vanni (1593). The
pictorial decorations of the
pillars and the 16th century
marble floor are very interesting.

THE CRYPT — In the photo above, on the left, one can see the crypt used as partial foundation of the temple. It is large and luminous and has a cross-vault and ample modern glass windows made by Fiorenzo Joni. On the main altar there is a very precious cross painted by Sano di Pietro. Other interesting works are a painting of Sodoma and assistants, representing « The Eternal Father and 4 saints », a painting representing the Madonna, attributed to Paolo di Giovanni Fei or to Francesco di Vannucci (second half of the 14th century), and a « Crucifixion and Saints » by Ventura Salimbeni. Below, on the right side: a wooden crucifix recently found in the crypt. The plaster covering it, was removed by a friar. This work of an unknown artist, is very valuable and dates back probably to the 14th century.

CHIGI SARACINI PALACE — It was begun in the 12th century and completed in the first half of the 14th century and many times restored during the following centuries. The Chigi Saracini Palace, once Marescotti Palace, is austere and graceful, magnificent and elegant at the same time. It is slightly bent in its front. It is made of stone and bricks with two orders of three-mullioned windows and a stone docked tower. Since 1932 it is the seat of the Chigian Musical Academy, an important centre for musical specialized studies, which every year, in July, organizes the Sieneses musical week. From the dark passage-way leading to the picturesque courtyard, one gets into the palace, which has very beautiful rooms, precious furniture, and interesting music-halls with a collections of ancient musical instruments. Many works of art, some of them very valuable, are kept in it.

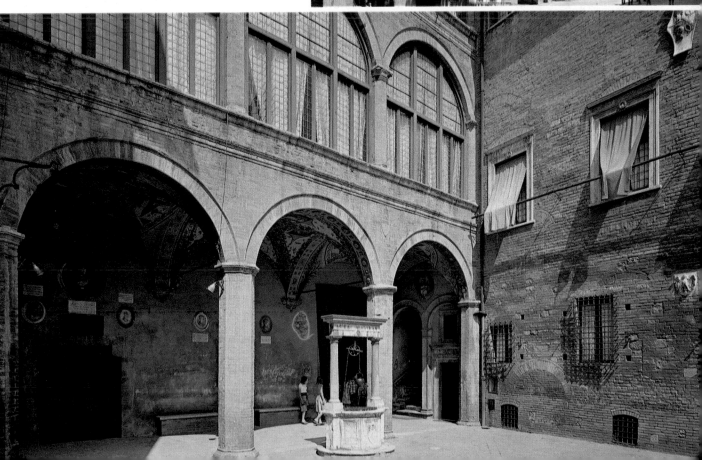

SALIMBENI SQUARE – This square, quiet and not very large, is enclosed on three sides by monumental palaces. On the background there is the front of Salimbeni Palace. It is a 14th century Gothic building, enlarged and restored in 1879 by Giuseppe Partini. It consists of three floors, of which the middle one is adorned with six elegant three-mullioned windows surmounted by ogive arches bearing the coat-of-arms. This palace is the seat of the oldest Italian credit institution, the « Monte dei Paschi di Siena », founded in 1472. On the right side of the square there is the Renaissance Spannocchi Palace, begun by Giuliano da Maiano in 1470 for Ambrogio Spannocchi, treasurer of Pius II, then completed by Partini in 1880. The ashlar facade presents, below, some rectangular windows and, above, two orders of mullioned windows. In front of it there is Tantucci del Riccio Palace, built in 1548.
In the centre of the square there is the monument to the economist Sallustio Bandini, made by Tito Scarocchi in 1882.

TOLOMEI PALACE – It existed already in 1205, but was completely remade after 1267. It is the oldest one of the Sienese private palaces. It is made of stone and presents, on the facade, two orders of rectangular mullioned windows surmounted by ogive arches, in which the trilobes are outlined. The Palace houses now the seat of the Saving Bank of Florence. In front of this palace, there is the church of St. Christophere of Romanesque origin, where the Council of the Republic used to meet before the Palazzo Pubblico was built.

The Walls and Gates of Siena

The mark of the communal culture, which has been kept intact through the centuries, characterizes even today this town, not noly in its monuments, but also in the whole area within the old city-walls. Dark and winding alleys among houses arranged according a very picturesque order, small sunny squares and narrow passage-ways, courtyards and archivolts connecting very near walls, streets sloping down till they meet in the centre of the town, in the large square of the « Campo », magnificent churches and houses, incomparable testimonies of culture and creative genius – this is the historical centre of Siena, the heart of a noble and gentle town, where all speaks of history and art.
Siena rises on three hills which, limited by the Arbia and Elsa, meet near the Campo (Field), taking so the shape of an upside-down Y. It is divided in three main districts called Terzi or Terzieri: the district of the Town, that of « San Martino » and that of « Camollia ». These main districts include some other smaler districts – the 17 « Contrade », each having its own flag, seat and church. All around Siena there are the powerful medieval walls about 7 kilometres long and including the many gates we can see in the photos on these pages.

CAMOLLIA GATE, built in the 14th century and re-built in 1604 on designs of Alessandro Casolani. It is situated to the north of the town and bears on the outside front of the arch an inscription welcoming the visitor: COR MAGIS TIBI SENA PANDIT (Siena opens her heart to you more than this gate).

ST. BARBARA FORT OR MEDICEAN FORTRESS – It was built in 1560 by Cosimo I. It occupies a quadrangular area and has robust towers on each corner. From the bastions, changed into public gardens in 1937, one can enjoy a wonderful view of the town and surrounding hills.

PISPINI GATE – It is the old gate of San Viene, to which in 1326 the tower, attributed to Minuccio di Rinaldo, was added.

ROMAN GATE – This well fortified gate dates back to 1327 and keeps the only fresco made by Sassetta.

OUTER PORT – It consists of a high embattled portal, almost all in stone. It dates back to the 14th century and constituted the advanced fortifications of the town to the north.

FONTE BRANDA – It is the most famous one of the many fountains of Siena, already existing in 1081. It was later enlarged by Bellamino and remade in 1246 by Giovanni di Stefano. Probably it was so called after a nearby house belonging to a certain Brando or Ildebrando, or else after an old Brandi family. It is made of bricks and has on its front three large ogive arches, surmounted by gables and adorned with merlons and four leonine gargolyes with the emblem of Siena in the middle. The fountain is dominated by the apse of the basilica of St. Dominic.

Catherine Benincasa (1347-1480) lived in this house, with its beautiful Renaissance portal in stone and a fine brick loggia. Catherine vigorously expressed the necessity of a deep renewal in the Church. She was canonized by Pius II in 1461 and in 1939 was declared by Pius XII patron saint of Italy. In the 15th century the house of Catherine was transformed into a sanctuary. Below: the Portico of the Italian Free Cities – double outside loggia, a part of St. Cahterine's Sanctuary, built in 1941.

State Archives

The State Archives are in the important Piccolomini Palace, the most beautiful building of Siena, begun in 1469 by Pietro Paolo Pirrina, probably on designs of Bernardo Rossellino.

The Archives, constituted in 1775 and placed in 1855 in the same palace, includes a large collection of records, which are very important for the knowledge of the Political, civil and artistic life of Siena and the whole province. They include parchments, more than 60.000 since the year 736, various laws of the Republic, letters and acts of the financial and judicial administration. The most interesting part of the collection has been arranged in three halls. It includes records concerning events and people mentioned by Dante in his Comedy; imperial credentials and papal bulls, the will of Giovanni Boccaccio, autographs and letters of famous men and women, artists, and records concerning famous works, such as the « Maestà » of Duccio, The Fonte and the Pulpit of Nicola Pisano. There are also commercial records and records concerning the Sienese studies, the Medici, the siege and fall of the town and the Palio. There is also an interesting collection of miniated statutes, such as the so called « Caleffo dell'Assunta » of Niccolò di Ser Sozzo Tegliacci (1334) and the « Statute of Merchandise », miniated by Sano di Pietro in 1472. Very precious from the historical and artistic points of view are the « Tablets of Biccherna », of which we reproduce here ten specimens, with the permission of the Ministry of Cultural and Environing Goods and of the State Archives of Siena. This collection consists of painted tablets used to cover, every six months, the books of the administrations of « Biccherna » and « Gabella ». The magistrates whorun the main financial offices of the Republic, changed every six monhts. At the end of their term they had their coats-of-arms and a sacred or symbolical scene commemorating the most important event of that period, painted in the wooden cover of the books. These tablets dated from 1268 to 1659, were painted by the most renowned masters of that time, such as Ambrogio and Pietro Lorenzetti, Giovanni di Paolo, Vecchietta, Sano di Pietro, Francesco di Giorgio Martini, Neroccio di Bartolomeo Landi, Domenico Beccafumi; just to mention only some of them. Apart from those of Biccherna, in the Archives there are also other tablets belonging to the books of the Hospital of « Santa Maria della Scala » and various Sienese institutions.

« Mystical Marriage of the Sts. Catherine of Alexandria and Catherine of Siena ».
Domenico Beccafumi – January-December 1548. This work represent the Mystical Marriage, showing the Madonna seating while the Child Jesus puts the rings on the fingers of the two Virgins keeling on his sides. At the lower centre there is the coat of arms of the Camarlingo Marinelli and other coat of arms of noble families.

« The Administration of Justice »
It was made by unknown author who received 30 « soldi » for his work. It refers to January-June of the year 1237. It was made at the time of Taddeo, Count of Urbino, of Montefeltro, mayor of Siena during the first semester of 1273. In the upper part are painted the coats of arms of the four Purveyors in charge. Enea di Rinaldo Piccolomini was Camarlingo « pro tempore ». In the lower part, we see the Mayor condemning a citizen. The administration of Justice was one of the few tasks of the Mayor after the institution in 1252 of the office of Captain of the People.

« The Good Governmnet of Siena »
Ambrogio Lorenzetti – July-June 1344 – The Good Government is represented by an austere and dignified figure. The four letters: C(ivitas) S(enarum) C(ivitas) V(irginis), that means « The Town of Siena is the Town of the Virgin », placed on the sides of the head, show the devotion of Siena to the Virgin to whom all the people offered themselves in order to ask her protection during the battle of Monteaperti. The coats of arms belong to the Forteguerri, Mignanelli and Ranuccini families, to which belonged the three Executors in charge, mentioned in the inscription.

« Don Ghiffolino Nazi, Abbot of San Donato, Camerlingo ».
◄ Coats of arms of four Purveyors – January-June of the year 1263. Unknown author: it is a copy of the original once belonging to the Ramboux collection of Colonia and sold in 1867. The name of the owner of the original is unknown. This composition represents the coats of arms of the four Purveyors in charge, whose names are mentioned in the inscription placed on the upper part of the tablet.

« Tax-collector and Tax-payer ».
Attributed to Ambrogio Lorenzetti. January-June 1340 — It was made at the time of Rinaldo Cimi of Staffolo, mayor of Siena in the first semester 1340. In this painting is represented the Camerlingo while receiving money from a tax-payer.

« The Woman with a gold-embroidered mantle ».
Taddeo Bartolo – 1421. In order to control the luxurious life of that time, which caused the ruin of many families, it was forbidden to wear velvet and silk or gold and silver embroidered dresses, except on special occasions. The so called « Tre Segreti », probably three secretaries had a book in which was a special mark. This tablet is the cover of the first one of these books, represented by a Sienese lady with a gold-embroidered mantle.

« The Circumcision of Jesus »
Attributed to Lippo Vanni – January-June 1357 — The painting represents Jesus in the temple to be circumcised. The coats of arms are of the families of the four Purveyors: Ughetti, Venturi, Ugurgeri and Salimbeni.

« The restored Government controls the citizens »
By an unknown artist – January-June 1385. The Sienese Republican Government, called in this period the « Concistoro », was also named after the number of the members of the « Concistoro ». So there was the Government of the Tirthy-six, the Nine, the Fifteen, the Twelve, etc. In 1385 came to power the Government of the Ten, which continued in office till Dicember 1387. This painting expresses the deside of having a stable government in Siena, after the revolution caused by the Emperor Charles IV, who came to Siena in 1355.

« The Camarlingo washes his hands while the Virgin protects Siena ».
Sano di Pietro – January-December 1451 – During 1451 the general council of the Republic took the necessary measures to control better the way of life of the public officials.

« The coat of arms of the Works Department of the Cathedral supported by two angels ».
Lorenzo di Pietro, called Vecchietta – 1434 – This tablet comes from the archives of the Works Department of the Cathedral of Siena and was the cover of one of the inventories there kept. This was the cover of a register of the rich patrimony of the hospital, including houses, shops, etc., which it let to various people and institutions.

The "Palio of the Contrade,,

Though we do not know much about the origins of the Palio of Siena, it is certain that this feast, the most popular and famous one of the town, existed already in 1310, when a document of the General Council of Siena officially instituted the Palio to be run on August 16th in honour of the Blessed Virgin. Originally the Palio which took place in the middle of August was only the crowning of a popular feast, after the battle of Monteaperti in 1260, with the victory of the Sienese people over the Florentines, it became ever more important and had a political meaning. In fact, by offering candles, they wished to honour the Madonna, to whom the people of Siena had consacrated themselves, and at the same time to confirm the autonomy and indipendence of the Free Town. Only in 1656 a second Palio, the « Palio of the Contrade », which takes place on July 2, in honour of the Madonna of Provenzano, was officially approved. The Sienese Contrade (districts) are practically the result of the decline of the central government in the Middle Ages. This situation brought people to rule themselves and join various associations. In the 13th century the Contrade were about 80, but gradually their number decreased and now they are only 17. Today the Contrade do not have only a representative function and their activity does not end with the Palio. Rather, we can say that in the present feverish world their vitality has a particular significance. Each Sienese is so tied to his contrada that we can say that the individual lives for the

community and the community takes care of the individual specially on the most important occasions of his life. The life of the Contrada is very intense for twelve months, but specially during the days of the Palio, when a suggestive feast has to be prepared. As a matter of fact, the Palio is more than a simple folk show or a historical celebration in costumes. Today as yesterday the Palio is the feast of Siena and Its 17 contrade, which fight for the painted silk drape. It is practically a rite, in which Siena since the drawing of lots, four weeks before the race up to the moment when the horses enter the arena for the final crazy race, shows its true face and relives with enthusiasm and nostalgic passion a wonderful dream of a splendid past. The crazy race lasts only a moment and is the most exciting part of the Palio. It is preceded by the picturesque parade, which coming from the courtyard of the Government Palace, in the Cathedral quare, enters the Campo, transformed for this occasion into a arena, which is unique of its kind. The Parade, animated by the splendid costumes and the sound of drums and the surprising flag waving, moves slowly along the track. It is an incomparable commemoration of the life and greatness of the ancient Republic. And Siena could not offer a more suggestive and proper scenery for it.

The Historical Parade opens with six mace-bearers and the flag-bearer of the Municipality, on horse-back with the white and black flag, called the «Balzana», which is the emblem of Siena. After the trumpeters and the musicians of the Palace, come the flag-bearers of the Towns, Lands and Castles which formed once the State of Siena; then the flag-bearer and the three Magistrates of Merchandise and the representatives of the major arts. The three Centurions of the Districts (« Terzi ») of the Town and of the Districts of Masse follow the Captain of the People. Then come the « comparse » of the ten contrade which run, all in the

The Major Page
of the Noble Contrada of the Eagle.

The Leader
of the Contrada of the Owl.

colourful costumes of their contrade; they are a drum-bearer, two ensigns, a captain, four pages, a flag-bearer, a jockey on horse-back and the so called « barbaresco » who leads tho race-horse. After the ten « comparse » of the seven contrade which do not run and the Captain of Justice, comes the Triumphal Chariot which, richly painted, bears the Palio which the winning contrada will receive as a prize, the white and black « balzana » and a small bell, called « Martinella ». Even the horse-men of the six contrade which now do not exist, take part in the Parade.

The Jockey with the Footman of the Contrada of the Tower, the first one of the race.

The Major Page of the Contrada of the Porcupine.

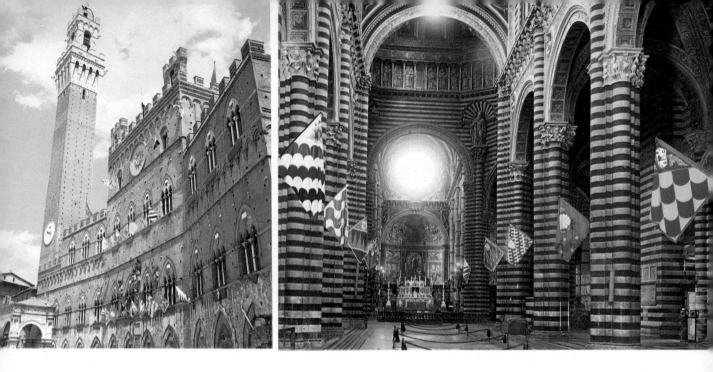

The Town Hall with flags and the blessing of the horse and jockey in the Oratory of the Contrada, on the afternoon before the race.

The Cathedral with the flags of the 17 contrade, on the occasion of the Palio which takes place on August 16. On July 2 the religious celebrations take place in the church of Holy Mary of Provenzano. Below, the Triumphal Chariot which closes the Historical Parade.

The Supper on the occasion of the General Rehearsal of the Contrada of the Tower. It is an important appointment for the Sienese, who take part in the feast, as it were a sort of collective rite, in the main street or square of the Contrada.

The Centurions of the « Terzi » in their colourful costumes; the Jockey with the Foot-man of the Contrada of the Giraffe and lastly the Pages of the Municipality bringing the Palio in the stand of the Judges.

In the photos of these pages there are some suggestive images of the final phases of the Palio. Above on the left: the rope (« canapo ») is on the point of falling down and the horses with their jockeys in simple costumes bearing the colours of their contrade, are waiting for the start. The Sienese Ensigns who are famous because they are very skilful in waving their flags, and the horses running a crazy race to win the Palio. It is a very exciting show, which rouses the enthusiasm of the Crowd of the spectators and makes new hopes and old passion relive, a show revealing the true and deep spirit of the Contrade. If the enthusiasm of the members of the Contrade is indescribable during the race, even more indescribable is the joy of those whose contrada has won. After a thanksgiving Te Deum in the Church of the Madonna of Provenzano on July 2 or in the Cathedral on August 16, they will carry the Palio along the streets of the town, while the drums go on rolling, the bells ring and flags are waved everywhere. Victory means also a great feast, which the members of the Contrada will conclude with the magnificent Supper of Victory.

CONTENTS

The Editor wishes to thank the Ministry of the Cultural and Environing Goods and the Direction of the State Archives of Siena for the permission to reproduce the « Tablets of Bicherma and Gabella » there kept; the Direction of the Works-Department of the Cathedral; the Municipality and all the other civil and religious institutions for the permission to take photographs.

L. 3500